The First Firefly

Books by Melville Cane

Co-Editor

The First Firefly

*New Poems
and Prose*

Melville Cane

Harcourt Brace Jovanovich, Inc., New York

Printed in the United States of America

Some of the material in this volume appeared
originally in *The American Scholar*.

Library of Congress Cataloging in Publication Data
Cane, Melville, 1879–
The first firefly.
I. Title.
PS3505.A557F5   818'.5'209   73–16006
ISBN 0–15–131280–x

First edition

B C D E

For my invaluable friends
Adolf and Beverley Placzek

Contents

The First Firefly

A Kind of Sound

I sit on a shaded porch,
inactively serene.
It's a hundred yards from the road;
a meadow's in between.
It's a soundless hour in June,
the random birds are still,
the sun is cordial and bland,
a book lies closed in the hand.

The faintest stir in the air
falls on a somnolent ear.
I'm not quite sure what I hear,
till it shapes, as it builds afar,
to the whir of a passing car.

Nightfall

Blue
thins.
Beige
dims.
Timidly,
out of the lilac hedge,
the first firefly
tentatively
tastes
and tests
the black.

Binny

The sun
is slipping;
evening's
drifting
in.

Stretched warmly at my feet,
Binny,
my terrier-friend,
sniffs,
and shares the deepening mood
of quietude.

We rest akin.

Autumnal

These leaves, once filled with chlorophyl,
must soon submit to Nature's will,
and with the earliest deadly frost
their verdant color will be lost,
to be replaced by carotene
as well as anthocyanin.

In other words, more simply told:
Wake up some day and you'll behold
the maples, proud in rose and gold.

Portrait

Her face is a hard dry mask,
earth in early March.
Under and over something passes,
Spring wind in sunlit grasses.

December Scene

Now in the cloudless icy air
a silver inchworm
stretches across the Colorado heaven—
United Air Lines
747.

Changing Rooms

At the hospital
the invalid
moved
serenely,
philosophically,
from TERMINAL
to eternal
CARE.

On Escaping a Mortal Illness

The Irresist-
ible Reaper,
eyes ashift,
missed
a tuft.

Tuning Up

Casually,
from either side of the stage
they straggle in,
carrying, dragging
cellos, contrabasses, tubas,
harps, bassoons and kettledrums,
picking paths to designated chairs.

Silence!

The concertmaster
enters,
fits his fiddle,
finds the key,
fixes the pitch.

They scrape and toot and strum and thump,
competitors in cacophony.

True soloists at heart,
but separatists no longer,
they orchestrate together
to share a single goal:
to lift the organic whole
to crystal harmony.

Scholarly Research

It was Mark Twain who once found it necessary to protest that a newspaper report of his death had been grossly exaggerated.

I was recently reminded of his remonstrance by the receipt of a letter, which I will produce with complete accuracy, my only amendment being to substitute fictitious names for the real ones. In so doing I have followed the example of Jack Webb, who on his television show, "Dragnet," a series based on actual crimes, always assures his public that the amendment has been made "to protect the innocent."

The letter, on the stationery of a western state university, is signed by a "Professor of English," whose research has unearthed not only my home address but the correct zip code numerals as well. I now reproduce it in full:

Oct. 8, 1972

Melville Cane Estate
400 E. 57th Street
New York, N.Y. 10022

Dear Sir,

In connection with a book I am writing about Mrs. Rosalind Doe, I am trying to locate the papers of the late Melville Cane.

(I have been told that Mr. Cane died recently, although I have not seen any obituary of him.)

Mr. Cane may have corresponded with the Does, and I am trying to determine whether his papers contain any letters from John or Mrs. Doe. If they do, I would like to obtain a xerox copy of each.

I would be grateful for any information that might lead me to Mr. Cane's papers.

Could you give me his exact date of death?

Thank you.

Sincerely,
Alden E. Ferguson

I felt that Professor Ferguson's letter called for prompt attention, and, in the interest of sound scholarship, at once responded:

October 12, 1972

Dear Professor Ferguson:

In answer to your letter of October 8th, addressed to my estate, I can well understand your inability to discover any published obituary since newspapers never, except by mistake, print such notices in advance of the event. They don't encourage that kind of scoop.

Similarly, the exact date of my death remains uncertain. It would be a great convenience if I possessed that information to pass on to you as well as to others who may be concerned.

Finally, I never corresponded with either Doe.

Yours,
Melville H. Cane

Our correspondence apparently has ended.

Footnote to Genesis

Adam, when he parted
with a rib,
had no idea he'd started
Women's Lib.

*

They'll equal be,
with women in,
but will they lose
what's feminine?

Mysterious Stranger

The man's approach was less than open;
his sentences would trail, half-spoken.
Resorting to the circumspect,
as though he feared to come direct,
he dealt in innuendoes
and double-entendoes.

The Little Boy

(After the return from Peking and Moscow)

The little boy
was shrewd and sly;
he always managed
to get by,
and after he
had risen high
and scanned the
advantageous sky,
he still pursued
his youthful game
and played it
pretty much the same,
and, finding the
old method worked,
he, smug with
satisfaction, smirked;
"How marvelously smart am I."

Conversing with Jung

These items are taken from my notes of talks with Dr. Carl Gustav Jung at his home at Küsnacht, Switzerland, in July, 1926, and during his seminar at Bailey Island, Maine, in the summer of 1936, following the receipt of an honorary degree at the Harvard University tricentennial commencement.

As long as there's a desire in man to explain himself, he will be saved from insanity.

Libido is the desire to move and live; one must desire and hope.

Libido comes from the solar plexus, *i.e.*, the sun; not the bright light of the sun but the dark light below.

Solemnity and grotesqueness don't hurt each other; grotesqueness belongs to the earth.

In daily life you can't be a believer in Dionysus.

If we're afraid of a thing it happens.

When you concentrate upon a thing, you have the capacity to change it. Concentration is preliminary to transformation.

Intuition tells of possibilities, sensation tells of realities.

Intuition does not say what things mean, but scents their possibilities. Meaning is given by thinking.

15

There's Danger in Candor

It clearly appears,
the gentleman fears
a danger
in candor,
whenever the truth is permissive.

How cozily safer
to set up a buffer
that's warranted "tightly repressive"!

Upton Sinclair
and the Ludlow Massacre

Upton Sinclair became a client of our firm through his friendship with my late partner, Bernard Ernst. They had first met as fellow-students at the College of the City of New York near the turn of the century; later they moved up to Columbia University to attend the famous graduate courses of Professor George Edward Woodberry in Comparative Literature; their intimacy grew through the ensuing years.

With a single exception, it was Ernst who handled Upton's legal matters until illness made that no longer possible. The single exception was due to the respective roles we assumed in our partnership arrangements; generally speaking, Ernst preferred office work, while I would take care of any litigation, cases for trial, and appeals in the courts.

It was early in 1914 that my turn to serve Sinclair arrived. Gentle and peace-loving throughout his life, he had been represented in a news story that morning as an advocate of violence to the point of homicide. The article had been concocted out of a reporter's imagination and was so damaging to Upton's reputation and character as a humanitarian that in self-defense he felt compelled to seek redress at law. There was no question in my mind, after reading the article, that he had a strong case; I so advised him, and received his authorization to take the necessary steps in a suit for libel.

The events that culminated in the libel are worth recalling, since they form a dramatic and momentous chapter in the war between capital and labor early in the present century. Historically the encounter is known as the Ludlow Massacre.

Ludlow was a small coal-mining town up in the Colorado Rockies. The mines were owned by the Colorado Fuel and Iron Company, a corporation of the Rockefeller family. There were "coal camps," as Sinclair related in his autobiography of 1962, "fenced in and guarded like medieval fortresses. No one could enter without a pass or leave without another, and the miners and their families were, in effect, slaves. When their appeals were turned down, they went on strike as members of the Western Federation of Miners, were evicted from the settlement, and set up tents in the nearby valley. The strike ran on with no ending in sight. Then one night, without warning, the management in retaliation ordered its goons to set fire to the tents.

"Three women and eleven children had been burned to death but the newspapers of the country, including those of New York, had given only an inch or two to the event."

When Sinclair learned who was responsible for the outrage he tried to see John D. Rockefeller, Jr., at the Standard Oil Building on lower Broadway, New York City, but without success.

As the news of Rockefeller's cold refusal to accept any responsibility spread, the determination of Sinclair and his group of protesters to seek whatever redress was possible grew more organized and pointed. A confrontation having been rejected, they were driven to a form of picketing. They proceeded to march in the formation of a funeral procession, back and forth, silently, past the entrance to No. 32 Broadway, until ordered by the police to "break it up."

Since they were neither disorderly nor blocking the sidewalk, they ignored the warning, and were promptly carted off to a police court, where, despite their insistence that they had broken no law, Sinclair and four female fellow-marchers were sentenced to a $3.00 fine each or to three days in jail. The five chose jail. Sinclair took advantage of his stay in the Tombs to go on a fast—"I had learned about fasting, and when I contemplated prison fare, I decided this was a good time to apply my knowledge." By the end of the second day, finding no further satisfaction from the experience, he paid his dollar for the final day of his sentence, and, once again a free man, proceeded to widen the area and intensity of his campaign.

His first move was to go out to Colorado to dramatize the inhuman conditions at Ludlow in speeches across the state, and by articles which the local newspapers could no longer ignore. Having succeeded in creating a favorable statewide public opinion, he returned to New York City to continue the fight.

Meanwhile, in his absence, the movement had grown beyond his control to include militant radicals and students of the Ferrer School, an anarchistic institution. Their next move, soon put into effect, was to shift the scene from lower Broadway to the Rockefeller estate in Pocantico Hills, Westchester County.

Although their approach had been peaceable—their request was simply to hold a free-speech open-air meeting on the grounds—the gates were locked against them.

It was only after the advancing marchers had been beaten up while staging a rally in nearby Tarrytown that they called on Sinclair, who had not been consulted over the expedition to Westchester, to head the movement and determine the next step.

Convinced that the acts of the police and the repressive attitude of the village fathers had clearly raised the vital issue of freedom of speech, Sinclair consented at once. Providentially—and ironically—he was backed by a liberal "millionaire lady whose estate adjoined the Rockefellers'," and who offered him the use of her open-air theatre for a public meeting.

These cumulative events—the Tarrytown set-to, the return of Sinclair to leadership, and his support from the millionaire society lady—brought the press post-haste to the scene, to take down Sinclair's address to the assembled countryside on private property. These colorful circumstances surely encouraged the hope of filing a dramatic story, since anything might happen.

The Sinclair speech proved sadly disappointing to the man from the New York *Herald*, who had apparently been counting on a rabble-rousing free-for-all. Instead, the ever-increasing crowd frequently broke into applause as Sinclair movingly unfolded the tale of the Ludlow Massacre, and pleaded for the correction of anti-labor abuses at the mines. He closed with a fervent, ringing appeal for justice for the helpless and underprivileged, not merely at Ludlow but throughout the nation.

Seemingly, the spirit of the occasion and the words of one of America's leading socialists and pacifists had made it impossible to write the true story for a newspaper committed to a capitalistic editorial policy. And so, the bewildered reporter, on telephoning for instructions was told to slant the facts to fit that policy. To do so called for a rich exercise of the imagination. Collaborating with his city editor, he produced a piece which appeared in the *Herald* the following morning.

In the article Sinclair was depicted as a fiery demagogue inflaming his audience to wage a class war against the vested interests and, if necessary, to resort to battle and "assassination."

This malicious attack, emphasized by an inviting headline, was further magnified by the invention that the president of the Tarrytown board of trustees had denounced Sinclair in a public statement. When Sinclair showed the article to the president, he not only called it a downright lie but repeated his denial in a letter for Sinclair to be forwarded to the newspaper for correction. It was only after the letter was ignored and the accusation was repeated the following day that Sinclair, his demand for a retraction unheeded, was roused to action.

I at once drew the papers for a damage suit in libel and had them served on the *Herald*. Its lawyers answered with a sworn disclaimer of all our charges, and I placed the case on the court calendar for trial.

Over two years passed before our case worked its way toward the top of the long list. Trial was at last imminent, and the other side had made no overtures for a settlement. Meanwhile, I had notified my witnesses and was ready to go on. Then, to my chagrin, a telegram from Pasadena,

California, casually informed me that Sinclair was too busy to come east. (He never explained what prompted him to this singular conduct, and I never inquired.)

I confess to being, if not in a state of shock, at least in a state of bewilderment. How could I proceed without my star witness? Withdraw the case after so many hours of preparation?

I decided on a strategy. The opposing lawyer was ignorant of my client's defection. His cause had involved my feelings for justice as well as professional pride.

I determined, despite my weakened situation, to press for trial. When the case appeared on the day calendar and the other side requested an adjournment, I vigorously objected. And when the court denied his request, my adversary for the first time suggested the possibility of a settlement. Accordingly I agreed to a short postponement to permit us to get together. Next day I received an offer of $500, which I flatly turned down. I was then told that $500 was the limit imposed by Mr. James Gordon Bennett, owner and editor of the *Herald*, for adjusting any legal claim without his personal authorization. Then, I answered, they'd better get in touch with him at once if they really wanted to avoid a trial. "He's on his yacht somewhere in the Mediterranean," came next over the telephone. I replied that if they really meant business I'd give them an additional forty-eight hours to locate him and produce a substantial offer.

And, sure enough, the strategy worked. Within the time allotted, Mr. Bennett having apparently been reached, the $500 figure was raised to $2,500. I accepted with studied reluctance and jubilantly wired the result to Sinclair, who supposed I had dropped the case on receiving his upsetting telegram. We shared the victory fifty-fifty.

The Bow Tie: A Symbol

I am happy to report that bow ties are on their way back in style. For years I've toured the smart haberdashery district of midtown Manhattan in a futile quest for replacements to my aging stock, only to be reminded that "there's no demand for 'em nowadays" or "they went out a generation ago." As a survivor of that lamented group I take that explanation as a reflection on my antiquity.

My preference for this modest sort of neckpiece over its more showy and expensive alternatives is deep-rooted; it goes back to the prep-school years of the eighteen-nineties and was fostered at first by a cotton fabric, usually of a Scotch plaid pattern, and priced on itinerant pushcarts at twenty-five cents.

Aside from a more formal white cravat, prescribed by my father as an essential part of my Sunday ensemble, my attachment to the bow variety has persisted with fair constancy ever since. Moreover, it has progressively developed a concern for quality and a taste suited to the individual I happen to be. My selections have been rarely disapproved and were even admired on occasion—high praise indeed—by a properly fastidious wife.

The bow tie, as I contemplate it, takes on the characteristics of a national symbol. I associate it with an earlier, unostentatious time in the history of the republic when life was healthier and homelier, before we, as a nation, had become overaffluent, overambitious, and world-powerful. Whether my imagination has led me astray and the facts may be otherwise is of no consequence. The imagination must prevail over the historical as representing the superior truth.

I welcome the wearer of a bow tie in the hope he may still be carrying on the traditions of the American of the old school. Although statistics are unavailable, my guess would be that in any national poll the Democrats would prevail over the Republicans. It was Thomas R. Marshall, vice-president under Woodrow Wilson, who proclaimed with general approval that what America needed most was a good five-cent cigar. Mr. Marshall wore bow ties and voted Democratic.

In a practical way the bow tie, by its horizontal position, enjoys an advantage over its pendant competitors, little noticed, but of sartorial importance. It derives from the anatomic configuration of Homo sapiens, more particularly from the relation of the head to the torso. The head protrudes and overhangs, while within the intervening space the bow tie rests, sheltered. The long tie, on the other hand, is vulnerable to embarrassing spottings, caused either by the eater or by a careless waiter ladling a mayonnaise sauce. (It is considered bad form to tuck in a napkin across one's girth as insurance against such mishaps.)

My pleasure over the reappearance of the bow tie upon fashionable counters has, however, been diminished. Upon further examination of the product and the manner of its presentation in the public press, it is my considered view that the symbol I cherish has been seriously weakened, if not destroyed.

A recent two-column ad in the New York *Times* leads regretfully to this conclusion. It announces, with flamboyant illustrations, that "the big bow is back again in butterfly and teardrop shapes, in plaids, prints and solids, in pure silks and even cotton velvets," and, as a final selling point, that "*it may be clipped on.*"

My kind of bow-tie man would scorn a clip, for he would still have the full use of his finger muscles and be able deftly to produce a smooth knot and draw the ends equal.

Observation

Man prefers woman
precise
in her reasoning,
provided
she serves it
with spice
in the seasoning.

Memo for Maid

The bowl
with the stew
broke
on the stove.

Tin-Pan Alley Rhymes

To cuddle up with Angela,
a-glide upon a gondola
along a smooth lagoon,
beneath an August moon:

Beyond all question, this
is my idea of bliss.

Company at Breakfast

I screwed the lid
of the honey-jar
and missed the thread
I was twisting for.

Safe from the risk
of being spilt,
it took on the mask
of a human tilt,
a most decidely rakish tilt.

The "lid" became the familiar flat
and favorite slanting hat
of a welcome figure of mischiefry—

and there sat
Chevalier,
facing me.

Advertising Copy

The English of the boys
on Madison
falls far below the prose
of Addison.

Editor

Ezra Pound,
knife in hand,
cut out the "Waste"
to save the "Land."

Tribute

A toast to E. C. Bentley, who
contrived with wit and aperçu
a four-line verse called Clerihew,*
(but mastered by a very few).

* His middle name. "A satiric or comic poem usually in two couplets."
—Standard College Dictionary.

Parsonical

There once was an Anglican parson
who harbored a weakness for arson.

*

The reason
I mention
this person
is merely
to fashion
this verse on.

Amour Propre

By the merest chance, the other day I came upon a document not intended for my eyes and chilling to my self-esteem. It was the official record of my admission in the year 1966 to a certain hospital for a slice of surgery.

The artist who had removed the destructive tissues and thereby restored my physical well-being never knew how his work had been undermined by a wound to my ego, inflicted at the reception office six stories below the operating theatre.

Following my name, they had booked me as

"This 87 year old white male."

To the Editor

The writing of "letters to the editor" is a form of prose which, so far as I am aware, has never received critical notice or been the subject of a thesis for the Ph.D. degree. But since my reading wanders most unacademically, this popular field may have already been explored and its riches exploited.

It is, however, a lawyer's curiosity rather than the urge of a man-of-letters that prompts me to engage in this modest piece of research.

One asks, logically, what motivates the sender? What untoward circumstance must have bestirred him to break out of his routine and seek public expression and expose himself above his personal signature?

The incentives are many. They include, one might suggest, a desire to promote some worthy cause, possibly to oppose an editorial position, or merely to protest against pot-holes in the pavement left unrepaired and not even guarded. Psychologically, in less definable categories, the impulse may arise from a need to satisfy the ego by seeing one's name in print and triumphantly pasting the clipping in a family scrapbook to impress upon a later generation the importance (or self-importance) of its author.

No money passes between the parties to an unsolicited offering, which may be tossed in the wastebasket at will or, if accepted for publication, take on value if it appears on the same page with the editorials. In such cases, the matter may assume certain aspects, to be considered later, of a business transaction.

A letter department is a regular, popular feature not only of dailies like the New York *Times* but of major weeklies like *Newsweek* and *Time*. It carries on in the spirit of our democratic tradition of the old town meetings and the cracker-barrel forums down at the country store.

It is not generally known, though the principle of value was established in the English Court of Chancery over two centuries ago, that the writer of a letter retains forever the sole right to publish it and, upon his death, convey that right to his estate or to a legatee. The receiver, on the other hand, becomes the owner of the physical paper, which he is free to sell (and keep the proceeds), or even to destroy, as he chooses.

Thus it is that extremely expensive collections of letters, such as the Berg Collection in the New York Public Library, owe this value not to literary rights—the right to publish the contents of the letters—but to documentary rights.

Although this law of divided ownership has no application to our present case, where the writer not only surrenders his reserved right but hopes that it will be exercised, a relationship has been created which may require further dealings.

They may relate to choices of spelling, *i.e.,* "honor" in America, "honour" in Britain; correcting a factual error, removing a bit of slang inappropriate to the general tone, et cetera. Changes of this type would by implication be authorized without consultation. A question of possible libel in a word or phrase, however, should be submitted to the letter-writer before making any revision of the text.

In short, these implied authorizations should be limited strictly to matters of form and style. Whatever the practice may be—and it varies—I am opposed to any tampering with the subject matter of a letter after it has once been accepted, whether by the removal of passages or by the insertion of any additions.

I happen to be a recent victim of editorial presumptuousness. On President Nixon's statement in January, 1973, that he had achieved "Peace with Honor" in Vietnam, I sent the following letter to the New York *Times:*

> Peace with Honor? Isn't that a bit thick? Peace with Skill? Assuredly yes, and less flamboyantly and *self-righteously* [my present underscoring], but more realistically, "Peace With Hope."

When the letter appeared, it was mutilated by the disappearance of my carefully chosen adverb.

The foregoing blend of law and belles-lettres turns out to have been a pleasant interlude (from the Latin, meaning play). As such I trust it may prove acceptable.

Obiters

_____

Her weltanschauung
is cosmetic,
rather than
cosmic.

*

The atmosphere
of the current epoch
does not conduce
to produce
an epic.

*

In much of Dickens
bathos thickens.

*

The greater the speed
the smaller the space.

Thomas Wolfe: A Memoir

It must have been in the spring of the year 1928 that I met Tom Wolfe for the first time. He came to me by way of my friend Aline Bernstein, the noted stage designer and costumer for the Theatre Guild and other contemporary Broadway producers. One day she telephoned to ask whether I was willing to see a young writer who had just completed a draft of his first novel and who was in need of advice, probably both legal and literary.

She was appealing to me, she said, because of my connection with the publishing house of Harcourt, Brace and Company, as its lawyer and unofficial scout for authors of promise.

She had read the manuscript—every page of it—she went on, and was ecstatic over its rare qualities. Her guess, she concluded, was that as a writer, especially of fiction, he was destined to a great career.

Naturally, and regardless of these superlative credentials, I set the date for an interview at my office. Promptly at the appointed hour Wolfe was announced. My secretary held the door open to admit him, a six-and-a-half-foot, lumbering giant, struggling with two weekend suitcases, which he deposited on the floor beside him. We shook hands across my desk, as he contrived to adjust his bulk to a chair designed for a less portly frame. Whether in uneasy anticipation of our meeting or from physical discomfort, he paused a few seconds to get his bearings as well as his breath. Then, with a slight stutter, he began by thanking me and sketching out his background as a writer, ending with his enrollment in Professor George Pierce Baker's celebrated English 47 Workshop for budding playwrights, at Harvard.

Under Baker's stimulus his work had progressed to the point of earning full-dress productions at the Workshop. Despite this success, he had begun to doubt whether the drama was really the metier he was meant by temperament to pursue.

By this time he felt sufficiently at ease with me to elaborate on his problem.

"I haven't dismissed the theatre by a long shot," he explained, "or the thrill one gets from a hit on Broadway, but as I thought more seriously of the future, I became more conscious of the restrictions of the dramatic form. The necessary disciplines to deal with them I felt ran counter to my nature. I needed a less confining, more expansive medium to be freer to express what I might want to say. That's why I've turned to the novel. This is a complete first draft, but before starting to revise and present it to a publisher, I feel in need of professional suggestions. Aline was sure," he ended, "you could be of help."

He stooped to pick up one of the suitcases, placed it upon my desk, and snapped it open. It was jammed to the top with typed manuscript. "This is the first half," he said; "the rest is in the other one. May I leave them with you?"*

Noticing my hesitation, he quickly explained that of course he wasn't asking me to read more than a few sample sections here and there, merely enough on which I might

---

* Forty-three years after the event I am producing the substance of our dialogue. The exact words can only be approximated.

base a first-blush impression. However, as my eyes took in the formidable heap, I was not enticed by his concessions. It would still be an unpalatable chore, whatever of time and thought it might consume.

Nevertheless, as we regarded each other for several seconds without speaking, I felt unable to resist the earnestness, almost desperation, of his pressure; he apparently had counted too heavily on whatever my judgment might be.

I could not let him down. And so I told him I'd take a look as soon as I could get around to it, if he wasn't in too much of a hurry. I suggested he telephone me for an appointment in ten days or so. I warned him not to expect anything more weighty than an average reader's opinion, for I certainly didn't hold myself out as an authority.

My words, though guarded, evidently reduced his tensions as he smilingly thanked me and left.

With the passing hours, the sight of those two pieces of luggage I found increasingly depressing. For my own peace of mind I determined to tackle my commitment at once rather than have it hang over me for some later time. At the end of the afternoon I left the office carrying suitcase Number One for after-dinner investigation.

I picked up a generous handful for a first helping and before completing the installment was almost ready to go along with Aline Bernstein's exuberant valuation.

What struck me first of all was the driving, passionate force behind the writing, as unrestrained as a force of nature, the words gushing forth, like a spring torrent, bursting all barriers and overflowing river-banks.

But as I continued, page after page, the impact of that first keen enthusiasm abated somewhat, though it never wholly deserted me. What the manuscript lacked basically was a shape, a sense of relative values in the material as it unrolled, what was important losing its full effect by intrusions of the commonplace.

The chronicle, as with so many first novels, was essentially autobiography in the raw, with little feeling for structure in the narrative, or for selectivity in its recital. The author's chief concern, it seemed, was "to get everything down" as he ransacked his prodigious memory. The self-critical, editorial process was exercised only sparingly.

Despite these deterrents, my involvement persisted, my curiosity to read on carried over to a second full evening. Clearly, inherent resistance to this Whitmanesque performance, my prejudice against rhapsodic prose, must not override my belief in the virtues of the text. The writing was eminently civilized, with a personal style, and its cumulative tensions impressive.

And so, on Wolfe's return to the office, I could sincerely report affirmatively and encouragingly, while at the same time emphasizing damaging shortcomings, the most serious being the elephantine length of the book.

(I learned later that the two suitcases harbored over 300,000 words.)

Wolfe, for the most part, took kindly to my criticisms, but when it came to the question of compression he balked. He was sure no part could be cut out without causing a loss to the whole. Since his mind was closed on the issue, I felt compelled to return his manuscript.

In parting, I advised him on what I believed would be the reactions of any publisher to a work of such inordinate length. If it appealed to him after a quick look, he would then have to consider realistically—since he was running a business—what acceptance would involve. It would mean assigning an editor who would have to spend an indefinite stretch of time, exclusive of all other work, in the mere reading of the entire script, before tackling the task, in co-operation with the author, of whipping it into physical, publishable shape. In addition there would be the various services incidental to its manufacture, and the further expense, among others, of a substantial allowance for advertising what might turn out to be a two-volume production, a special problem in selling fiction.

At best, I ventured, the odds of even ultimately recouping the cost of the undertaking, let alone the possibility of a profit, would hardly warrant the venture. The reactions of the reading public, I explained, were decidely unpredictable.

As I wished him luck he thanked me, sincerely, I thought, but plainly with disappointment.

Up to a point my predictions were not wide of the mark. *Look Homeward, Angel* was submitted through an agent to several publishers and in each case was turned down. But in the end it found a reader willing to take the gamble and assume the responsibilities I had outlined to Wolfe; a reader with an uncanny sense for detecting talent though obscured by inferior craftmanship, plus a deep concern for furthering the careers of his authors. The man was Maxwell Perkins, chief fiction editor at Scribners, and mentor of Fitzgerald and Hemingway.

In Perkins Wolfe found a man sympathetic to his aspirations and expert in the skills for their attainment. The relationship developed well beyond the usual roles of editor and author; it became symbiotic, with Perkins' deepening involvement. He served as a participating collaborator in spirit, though never as a contributing co-author.

Look Homeward, Angel appeared the year after my first meeting with Wolfe and my experience with that enormous first draft. I recalled his disappointment over my unwillingness to recommend it for publication in its forbidding state. In retrospect, however, he must have come around to my view, since I was one of the earliest to receive a presentation copy. Attached to the title page was the following generous, undated letter:

Dear Mr. Cane:

You were one of the first people who said a good word for this book and I hope you will like the job Scribner's and I have done in revising it.

I know you are a very busy man, but I wish you could read all of the 626 pages. If you can't, try to read every other one.

Thanks very much for all your help, advice, both personal and legal. All of it helped me, and I hope to show the good effects in my next book.

Faithfully,

Tom Wolfe

Perkins had succeeded—I could identify with his unequal struggle—in reducing the opus, still magnum, by almost fifty per cent.

Years after Wolfe's death I received further evidence of the importance he attached to his meetings with me. I found it in two published letters, the first to a friend, George Wallace, dated June 25, 1928, in which he writes:

Mr. Melville Cane, attorney for Harcourt-Brace, says it's a *good* book—a fine, moving and distinguished piece of writing. . . . If I cut, he thinks it will get published.

(He omits referring to my other requirements besides cutting.)

The second reference occurs in one of a series of letters to his old high-school teacher, Mrs. Margaret Roberts, published in *The Atlantic Monthly* and written in a state of blissful delirium over the acceptance of *Angel*. His estimate of my professional attainments is, understandably, unreliable.

Jan. 12, 1929

Dear Mrs. Roberts:

Scribners have already signed the contract. I am to sign it Monday, but with their customary fairness they have advised me to show it to a lawyer before I signed. I am therefore going with Mrs. Boyd [his agent] to see Mr. Melville Cane, a lawyer, a poet, and a member of Harcourt-Brace & Company, and the finest attorney on theatrical and publishing contracts in America. I have met him once, he read part of my book and he has since been my friend and well-wisher. He told the person who sent me to him some time ago that I represented what he had wanted to be in his own life, and that I was one of the most remarkable people he had ever met. And when he was told yesterday that I had sold my book, he was delighted.

(The contract was more than fair; it was generous. Scribners limited its rights to publication in book form and, contrary to prevailing practice, claimed no share in so-called "subsidiary rights," such as dramatic, motion picture, and foreign.)

Despite these signs of appreciation and allegiance, Wolfe was never a consistently steadfast client, as was the case with Sinclair Lewis and other authors. I doubt this was calculated, but due, rather, to innate fickleness and inconstancy of character. I learned of his having consulted other lawyers on at least two occasions, one concerning the recovery of stolen manuscripts and, more important, when he and Scribners were both sued for a libel arising out of one of his short stories.

Yet, in the long run, and down to the end, he would return.

Not long after the publication of *Look Homeward, Angel,* Wolfe had me draw his will, which he left with me for safekeeping. It was a simple instrument, its main provisions being the division of his estate equally between the two persons then deepest in his affections, his mother and his benefactress, Aline Bernstein, and the appointment of Maxwell Perkins as executor.

At the time of its execution the very existence of an estate was hypothetical; the impulse which drove him to an act so uncharacteristically businesslike indicates his self-confidence in the rewards his future writings might earn.

Following *Look Homeward, Angel,* Wolfe set to work on another novel, which eventually, after some five years of false starts and other frustrations, he completed and entitled *Of Time and the River.* In the summer of 1930, feeling the need of a change of scene as a therapy for the confusions that continued to block him, he decided on a trip to Europe.

Before leaving New York he dropped in to say good-bye, and I suggested he look up my friend William Aspenwall Bradley, who had established himself in Paris as an international literary agent, and who might prove to be of use. In any case, he would be good company.

The following letter, dated July 22, 1930, came from Hotel Lorius, Montreux, Switzerland.

Dear Mr. Cane:

Thanks very much for your note and excuse my lateness in answering it. I did not get to see Mr. Bradley in Paris—I think he was not in town. I am staying here in a very beautiful place—I have a good room with a big balcony that looks out on a magnificent garden and Lake Geneva. I am working several hours a day; if I have talent and strength of will enough to put my book down as I have it inside me, I think it will be good. . . .

I hope this finds you well and in good spirits and I send you my best and warmest wishes.

Ever yours,
Tom Wolfe

In the years to follow the writing of *Of Time and the River*, I would run into Tom from time to time at some social affair or we might meet by chance on the street and stop for a talk. Our relations remained friendly, though no more intimate than in the earlier days. Meanwhile, he had gained a solid reputation through the two novels as one of the younger writers to be reckoned with, and he profited by the controversies of contending admirers and those who were disaffected, as they aired their views at cocktail parties and in the literary magazines.

He was hard at work, he told me at a later time, but for the present was not ready to venture on another long novel. Instead he inclined to the shorter forms, stories and novellas, while also piling up a mass of miscellaneous material for possible future use in the longer form.

I had been following his work in *Scribner's* and other magazines and was especially impressed with a novella, "I Have a Thing to Tell You," which had appeared in *The New Republic* in March, 1937, and which explored fresh territory, Nazi Germany and the fate of a German Jew, a fellow-train-passenger, in his vain attempts to escape to freedom.

Wolfe, I felt, had grown in both outlook and sympathies in the creation of a character and a situation far removed from the world of the Gant family. The tale also marked a decided advance in organization and a gain in technical skill. What pleased him most was that I stressed his progress as an artist. His chief and constant concern, he said, was to be able to control "all those words" and not be their captive.

One evening following the appearance of "I Have a Thing to Tell You," my wife and I were finishing dinner at a French restaurant in the East Fifties and were about to leave when Wolfe entered alone, and, catching sight of us, made for our table. His greeting, I felt, seemed heartier than our intimacy warranted, and he stuttered as he started to speak. He was preparing to sit down and join us when we rose, regretting we were already late for an engagement.

At this he became unaccountably excited. He had been meaning to consult me for some time on an important matter, and he insisted we must get together for an evening as soon as I could make it. As his voice rose and people were turning our way, to avoid embarrassment I did fix a time and place, trusting he would forget it.

But it didn't work out as I had hoped. The day before our appointment he telephoned to confirm it.

The place was Cherio's, a favorite hangout for writers and publishers in the late nineteen-thirties, on Fifty-third Street, east of Madison Avenue. When I arrived he was already standing at the bar, waiting. As we sat down to eat, I concluded that his stand at the bar must have been of some duration, for he was in a highly agitated state and at times incoherent. As the evening wore on it became clear that our meeting was not in the least professional but that I had been tricked into serving as a convenient receptacle for the endless outpourings of his grievances.

The grounds for his disturbed state have been examined into and argued over by scholars and critics so exhaustively that they require no lengthy consideration here. They form the basis of a famous chapter in the history of American publishing, the story of Wolfe's break with Scribners and especially of his rejection of Perkins, as both editor and faithful adviser. Of the emotional currents at work, two factors stand out: Tom's growing obsession that the firm was old-fogy and his fixation that Perkins had ceased to be the stimulating and helpful father-figure and now was hampering his progress and hindering his freedom as a creative writer.

His truculent attitude toward the firm had turned to positive hostility; he had already written and published a devastating lampoon of one of its senior members and, losing

47

all sense of loyalty, was contemplating a more compre-
hensive and contemptuous satire.

The inevitable separation proved painful to all concerned.
It left Wolfe in a state of shock which incapacitated him
for productive work, destroyed his peace of mind, and ac-
counted for his disoriented behavior at the French restaurant
as well as his peremptory demand on my time. Seeing me
so unexpectedly must have stirred memories of earlier occasions when I was of use to him.

By the time I felt able to break away, he had fallen into
a more equable mood, having exhausted both his catalogue
of grievances and the effectiveness of his stimulants.

On parting he announced he wanted to make a new will,
and I suggested that he write out in advance whatever was
to be included. It was brief: the entire income from his
estate was to go to his mother for the rest of her life, and on
her death the principal was to be divided into four equal
parts for his two sisters and two brothers. Finally, what
seemed to register the end of his hysterics and mark the
return to sanity was his redesignation of Perkins as executor.

After the will had been witnessed he lingered on, relaxed
and evidently relieved that he had set his house in order.
As he rose to leave, he said—they were his exact words: "I'll
never again take an important step without consulting you
first."

I had seen Tom Wolfe for the last time.

Not long afterward I read in a literary column that he
had signed a long-term contract with Harper for his future
writings.

Soon he was heading for the Northwest. It was on this

trip with friends that he contracted an illness which ultimately developed into a brain condition, the result of an early, supposedly eradicated tubercular infection, which failed to respond to surgery. He died September 15, 1938, in his thirty-ninth year.

One is tempted to speculate, charitably, whether his erratic, disturbed personality at this time was in any way related to the persistence of this fatal malady over the years.

I notified Perkins that I had Tom's will, that it was made after the break, and that nevertheless he, Perkins, had again been named as executor. In answer to my question, he agreed wholeheartedly to serve, and asked me to do whatever was legally necessary to administer the estate.

At the time of Tom's death his bank balance was slightly over eight thousand dollars; it represented the rest of the ten thousand dollars he had received from Harper as an advance on the signing of their contract. The hidden assets, however, were stored in the unopened crates of manuscript, out of which his new editor, Edward C. Aswell, was to shape three full-length works of fiction, *The Web and the Rock*, *You Can't Go Home Again*, and *The Hills Beyond*.

Lawyer-Poet, Poet-Lawyer

(Introducing a poetry evening at the Association of the Bar of the City of New York, February 23, 1972)

Fellow Members and Friends of both poetry and law:

One morning shortly before last Christmas I picked out of the mail on my office desk an envelope bearing the name of an eminent, long-established law firm. I wasn't in a hurry to open it since I assumed it contained the usual seasonal appeal for a contribution to the writer's pet charity.

I was never more happily mistaken.

Instead of the expected request, the letter turned out to be a serendipity, one of those unforeseen windfalls out of the blue, and this one far more welcome than an improbable legacy from a remote relative with no cause to remember me.

It was signed Keith Highet, not in his professional capacity but as chairman of the section on law and the arts of this association; it was, in fact, an invitation, to quote his engaging phrases, to appear before you and "either to discuss the intermixture of a career as poet and a career as lawyer, or to read from some of your works and possibly add your own commentary or both. You would have an hour or more, if you wished, in which to regale us."

I read and reread the letter with conflicting emotions—first with disbelief, and then with gratitude, with amusement, and finally with self-importance. As I took in its full meaning, I concluded that far more than making a gracious gesture, Mr. Highet and his committee had officially certified me as having passed my bar examination as a poet. So here I stand, hoping as best I can to validate the award. The program will be an informal, somewhat ad lib variety show, a brief explanation of the "intermixture," many samples, with passing comment, of poems serious, light, satirical, and frivolous taken from two of my books, and possibly a piece or two of prose on the legal side. The two books are my latest, *Eloquent April*, published last year, and *So That It Flower*, a selection made in 1966 of some two hundred and forty poems I wished to preserve from earlier volumes no longer available.

But first the "intermixture," a well-chosen, accurate term to define the duality of the careers, since they do not function independently of each other but, on the contrary, make helpful, supportive crossovers. A fair example would be my use of conciseness, whether in writing a legal brief or in composing a lyric.

That a person should actually pursue two callings with dedication to each is regarded by the press and consequently the general public as a phenomenon out of the ordinary and therefore as newsworthy as the birth of quintuplets. From my experience with interviewers I know that their chief interest is numerical rather than in the forces that impel an involvement with more than a single strain or stream of one's personality.

The names of Wallace Stevens and William Carlos Williams, two pre-eminent American poets, are those usually cited as examples of this supposedly rare combination. Stevens, it is said, would compose lines as he walked from his home to his job as an executive of a Hartford insurance company. Williams was a physician, a pediatrician who by turns delivered verses and babies.

My own venture into what may be defined as a course in double-dealing was not undertaken until well into my forties. Meantime, starting with prep-school doggerel, I had, with discipline and craft, developed a vein that appealed to the college papers and such national outlets as *Puck, Judge,* the old *Life,* and F.P.A.'s column. My attempts in more serious fields were sentimental, derivative, and, as I look back, embarrassing.

Nevertheless I must have entertained the hope to create on a less ephemeral level, for I recall harboring the vague ambition to write a single poem worthy to be included in some future edition of Palgrave's *Golden Treasury.* This youthful fancy must have been inspired by my first experiment in genuine self-expression, a simple nature lyric which my mentor, Professor George Edward Woodberry, himself a poet, warmly endorsed as being, in his words, "the real thing."

Although encouraged by his commendation I was too bound by fixed habits and professional responsibility to engage in an undertaking so demanding and so foreign to the pattern of my life. It took many years before I dared summon enough self-confidence to face this neglected, dormant side of my personality. Reluctantly I learned to accept that egoism which is the necessary driving force of the creative artist.

The break-through came in the summer of 1925. With my wife's blessing I rented a shack at Ogunquit, Maine, overlooking the sea, and, alone and free from contact with the outside world, spent a full month in assembling and organizing material gathered over the years but left to lie fallow. By the end of my stay I had managed to shape a sufficient number of the better pieces to make a small book, which Donald Brace wrote that his firm "would be proud to publish." Its title was *January Garden*. Ten other volumes have since appeared.

(The readings, with comments, followed.)

The Closing Prayer

In a long life there come moments even the most insensitive individual is not apt to forget, particularly when memory is sharpened and intensified by the shock of the unexpected, the element of surprise. Being taken unawares tends to deepen the receptivity of the brain to record and retain, and therefore to recall the more minute and elusive details, to vividly relive the original drama.

It is an experience of this character I venture to reconstruct faithfully as can be, some seventy years after the event.

The setting is a Hebrew synagogue, Temple Emanu-El in the City of New York; the time, a day late in May in the year 1902; the occasion, the spring festival of Shabuoth or Pentecost; and the ceremony, the induction into Judaism of a group of boys who have reached their thirteenth year and, by ancient tradition, are deemed qualified to assume the duties and responsibilities of maturing adults.

For these boys it is Confirmation Day; for them and their co-educational sisters it also marks their graduation from Sunday school.

One of these confirmants-to-be, and the leading actor in the present chronicle, is my brother, younger by nine years, William Goodman Cane.

That Temple Emanu-El happened to be chosen for our religious schooling was to be expected since, almost from its beginnings on the Lower East Side, dating back to the middle of the nineteenth century, the family of my mother had been—and still were—active members and pewholders. The temple had steadily advanced over the years to become a major force in Reform Jewry throughout the United States; it had long since outgrown its early quarters, and was now magnificently established at the northeast corner of Fifth Avenue and Forty-third Street in an imposing edifice of Oriental dignity and splendor.

A further, sentimental influence to bind us to Emanu-El was my parents' marriage, performed in 1878 by its senior rabbi, now emeritus, the Reverend Gustav Gottheil.

The ritual for the celebration of Shabuoth included as a special feature participation of the confirmants, by joining with the choir in singing the hymns, and by their collective responses to the scriptural readings at the pulpit by the rabbi and the cantor. An especially important assignment was the delivery of the closing prayer of the service by that member of the graduating class with the highest scholastic record. The fortunate winner was also awarded an annual medal of honor, the gift of the president of the Congregation then in office. In the year 1902 he was James Seligman of the noted banking firm.

It was more than conscientious custom that drew us to the temple on that holyday morning. We were moved by family pride and affection, since the person chosen to deliver the closing prayer and to receive the medal was my brother, Bill.

The occasion, for me, took on a special involvement, since I was implicated, in a minor way, as an off-stage collaborator.

The closing prayer was a set piece in the ritual, unchange-

55

able through the years. Fervent and eloquent as an expression of youthful dedication, it demanded no originality of either thought or composition from the speaker, but called strongly for the exercise of his elocutionary gifts in a tone and spirit suited to the hour. It accordingly denied him the opportunity for personal revelation but limited him to the role of an actor, to read the lines handed him.

Since this was to be Bill's first appearance as an orator, he approached the task with the amateur's sense of insecurity and inadequacy. His first step would be to commit the piece to memory and to become so letter-perfect and self-confident as to bar out, so far as could be anticipated, either a sudden spasm of stage-fright or any verbal slips or slurrings.

Before starting out, in his innocence, he turned to me for brotherly instruction and to reap the benefits of my own experience, for it so happened that I, too, had been chosen for the same honors nine years earlier and had met the ordeal without disgrace. That made me, in Bill's eyes, an authority.

I agreed to serve as his coach and trainer and in due course saw him through countless hours, so it seemed, of trial and error up to the dress rehearsal for the great day.

Our sessions were difficult, often exasperating, for Bill's plodding progress at times taxed my patience and my pace to the degree of unfairness. After all, he was doing his faithful best, whereas I held the advantage of a dominating senior.

My chief endeavor was to rid him of mechanical singsong and to make him feel, and convey his feeling to the assembled worshippers, that he genuinely believed in the noble sentiments that passed through his lips. In this endeavor he became moderately plausible, but not before we had succeeded in overcoming certain troublesome drawbacks, one of which I still sharply remember.

It consisted in his unfortunate habit of placing false emphasis upon certain words while glossing over the importance of others. The consequence created a distortion of meaning. It took several sessions, for example, to straighten Bill out over the phrase "satisfaction and delight," to reduce his stress upon "satisfaction" and subordinate it to "delight," which, though more noteworthy in the context, he had trailed off into comparative obscurity.

On the matter of gestures we found ourselves in fair agreement: that they should be free from flamboyance, sparing in number, and be used only to enhance the effect of some demanding point of passage. By the end of our rehearsals Bill was employing gestures with proper economy.

All in all he was prepared to give a presentable account of himself. He possessed the further advantages of an agreeable presence and a voice well past the changing stage, which carried both volume and resonance.

The day, so long awaited, was at last at hand. All five of us, my parents, Bill, Stanley, our eleven-year-old brother, and I rose early, Bill a bit bruised from a fall down the stairs the previous evening—but sound in spirits nonetheless.

Services were scheduled to begin at ten o'clock, but we left our house on East Eightieth Street ahead of time, for Bill had first to join his classmates forming in the assembly-room below the temple.

As we approached our destination we could hear the thunderous tones of the organ rolling through the open doors into the bright spring sunlight of the noisy city. We entered and were ushered to our pew, which was well located on the center aisle though somewhat toward the rear.

Not too comfortably seated—it was a tight squeeze, for my father was a bulky man—we gradually eased in, as the choir of professional singers intoned the opening hymn. Simultaneously from an inner room at the other end of the temple four figures emerged to take their seats on the altar, two on either side of the Ark of the Covenant, which held the scrolls of the Torah or Pentateuch, the books of the Old Testament. Following these principals came the confirmants and graduates, the boys and girls in separate files. Of the four principals, two were present in an honorary capacity, Dr. Gottheil, now retired, and the president of the congregation, Mr. Seligman; the conduct of the services rested with the officiating rabbi, Dr. Joseph Silverman, complemented by the cantor, whose name now escapes me but whose devout, sonorous baritone, as he chanted the ancient melodies, I have never forgotten.

Dr. Silverman was tall and slender, his face framed by a brown ecclesiastical beard, probably in his late forties or early fifties. He had been called to Emanu-El from a less prestigious flock to assume the ministry on the retirement of the aging Dr. Gottheil. His appearance and bearing bespoke the dedicated preacher. He walked with a slight stoop to the body, as though wrapped in meditation, and he seemed by nature to be more like a shepherd caring for the spiritual needs of his congregation than one possessing the temperament and drive of a pulpit orator. He had already served one full term with credit, but when the time came in the previous year for his reappointment, he met with serious and unexpected resistance. The membership divided almost equally, the opposition favoring a more dynamic and dramatic personality, but after a sharp contest, his friends prevailed and he was voted in for a full second term.

My father had worked hard for Dr. Silverman, not only because he believed him deserving of re-election, but also on the ground of blood-brotherhood, for they belonged to the same fraternal lodge, a chapter of the Independent Order of B'nai B'rith.

Following the singing of the hymn with a prayer of welcome, the services proceeded in an atmosphere of moving solemnity. They were conducted, according to tradition, in two languages, English and Hebrew, the English part by Dr. Silverman, the Hebrew by the cantor. Their respective contributions interwove to form a mosaic of religious fervor and eloquence, further enriched by the accompanying music of organ and choir.

Presently rabbi and cantor strode slowly toward the Ark and opened it; the cantor removed one of the scrolls, carried it forward, unrolled it as he chanted various excerpts appropriate to the festival. After redepositing it, the cantor returned to his seat. The moment had arrived for the confirmation.

The candidates on either side of the altar rose, facing one another, as Dr. Silverman, standing between them, uttered with fatherly counsel the official words of initiation.

There then remained but two related events to be celebrated, before the final benediction: the delivery of the closing prayer and the bestowal of the Seligman medal.

Unexpectedly, however, the services came to a sudden

unscheduled halt. Dr. Silverman seemed unable to continue. He hovered bewildered, as if suffering from a temporary lapse of memory. Then, still speechless, with a single gesture of the hands, he dismissed the mystified confirmants, who stepped down from the altar to the joyous peals of the organ and then separated to return to their respective families.

Prisoned in our pew, we sat in stunned shock, as Bill, unspoken piece in hand, walked the long aisle to rejoin us. Upon our excited questions he was unable to throw the least light. It had all happened so swiftly, so upsettingly, that he had been struck helpless. As he spoke, my mother broke into quiet weeping, while Stanley held her hand. But my father blazed with fury and uncontrolled vilification, which rose above a whisper, despite my mother's nudgings for him to quiet down. A man easily given to outbursts of profanity, he denounced the rabbi, proclaimed he should be discharged for unfitness, and reproached himself for having supported his re-election. Plainly he was in no condition to deal with the situation.

I seethed in a similar though less violent state of distraction during my father's fulminations, when suddenly I felt the flash of an idea. Assuming the paternal role, I commanded Bill to return to the altar and notify Dr. Silverman of his blunder. The gathering was, fortunately, still in session; the four official personages were still seated on the altar; the choir were in the midst of the final anthem; the portals opening out to Fifth Avenue were still shut.

Bill obeyed on the instant, and seconds later had reached the altar, gained Dr. Silverman's eye, and reawakened his memory to the moment when it had failed him. He promptly rose, and, advancing to the pulpit, stated that he had to make the following announcement:

That as a departure from the customary order, it had been decided to postpone to the end of the service the recital of the closing prayer and the bestowal of the annual medal.

He then called Bill to his side and properly introduced him.

I admit to a deep concern over the outcome of what was to follow. I questioned whether Bill's nervous constitution was equal to bearing the burden of his ordeal. But my fears proved groundless. The turmoil, on the contrary, had stirred his blood, generated a determination to rise above the disappointment of a seemingly hopeless debacle, and invested his lines with an eloquence and conviction I had never been able to arouse. He had triumphed.

Dr. Silverman, with words of congratulation, then handed him the Seligman medal. The services were now at an end.

Proudly jubilant, we swept out of the temple, lingering only to absorb the congratulations of friends before boarding a Fifth Avenue stage for the trip home. All tensions had evaporated, my father's temperature had dropped to normal, as, contentedly, we settled down for the holiday banquet.

A Translation from the Russian

One morning not long ago I received an out-of-town call at my office; the voice was that of a stranger. He self-consciously introduced himself as an instructor of Slavic languages at an eastern university and after apologizing for breaking into my professional hours—he lacked my home address—he disclosed the object of his call. He was engaged, he explained, in compiling an anthology of modern Russian poetry in English translations and he hoped to induce me to join in the collaboration at least to the extent of half a dozen contributions. By way of assuring me of his literary solvency he hastened to inform me that he was proceeding under a contract from a publisher of consequence and that he had already received favorable replies from several poets whose work I chanced to hold in respect.

To so flattering and persuasive an invitation my reply was less than cordial. "I'm sorry," I said, "to have to say no, on several counts. I'm presently committed to my own work, I haven't attempted a translation since I toyed with Horace and Catullus in freshman year, and most important of all, I don't know a word of Russian, and, what's more, I hold a low view in general of translation as an art form."

I had laid it on fairly thick, in the hope of bringing the conversation to a quick end, but he was not to be so easily dismissed, and hung on, primed with counter-arguments.

"Oh, you'll have plenty of time for your own work," he began; "this won't interfere in the least. And you don't have to know any Russian. In fact, not a single poet on my list does." He mentioned two of the most currently prominent. "It gives them more leeway."

"That's a new concept," I said, "at least to me. The first qualification of a translator nowadays is ignorance of the original language?"

He brushed that aside without letting go.

"I know it sounds unscholarly, but please at least give me the chance to state my case."

He was so winning and earnest in his appeal that my curiosity became slowly awakened, though my aversion toward his theory and method remained untouched.

"All right," I said in a tone of gracious indulgence, "I suppose you're entitled to a hearing, that is, if you can find a Russian poem you think may be literature and not another piece of propaganda dressed up to look like verse."

"That will be easy"—his voice lifted—"I'll mail you a fair sample. You be the judge."

Instead, two mornings later, on arriving early at my office I found him sitting there, briefcase in hand.

"I hope you won't mind my pleading my case in person; it'll only take a few minutes." As he spoke he drew from the briefcase a set of notes, with a few selections of the works of two popular contemporary Russian poets.

"They're both in good standing," he explained, "and if you're interested enough to try your hand after hearing what I have to say, you are free to choose the one you'll be more comfortable with."

He handed me two carefully typed memoranda; the one consisted of a literal version of the poems in plain prose for their meaning; the other, in Russian characters, the originals, printed as they had appeared in the published volumes except that he had added short stresses to indicate where the emphasis should fall.

After reading each in turn I became sufficiently impressed with their content and treatment to be induced to take a gamble. So I read them a second time to choose the group more congenial to my own temperament. I returned the other set, saying: "If you're not too much in a hurry, I'll make a try; but if I find I'm not up to it, I'll notify you promptly so that you can find someone else in time."

He readily agreed, adding: "I forgot to say that we're placing no limits on your imagination, that is, so long as you stick to the form and don't alter the meaning."

With this further incentive, on the next weekend I took the poems, six of varying length and differing themes, with me into the country. My mentor's parting dispensation gave me a needed sense of freedom as it brought home the reason for my aversion to most translations in the past—their general lack of imagination.

I recalled especially in this connection the prosaic virtues emphasized in advertisements to attract buyers; the phrase "a faithful rendition," for example, suggested morality rather than art, as if the sole duty of the translator were to preserve the original in its uncontaminated verbal state.

Immersing myself in the poems as enjoyment grew, I awakened to the creative world of my Russian model and entered into a symbiotic relationship with him. He observed life with philosophic detachment, prepared to support his lyrical compositions with an obbligato of quiet humor.

I returned to the city, exhilarated with a bag of six, which

I sent off to my mentor for judgment and possible rejections. Suspense was brief. I had met his specifications and hopes, he soon wrote warmly, with only an occasional correction where I had gone astray, especially when I had attributed to a character an anti-Marxian dissent impossible in the Soviet Union.

The experience, as I look back on it, caused me to re-examine my position toward translation and to come up with fresh conclusions, the most essential being that to succeed as a work of art a translation of a poem should be undertaken, if not by a practicing poet, at least by a person possessed of the poetic impulse and the capacity for imagination. It should never be assigned to a linguist, however accomplished.

Sometime after this experience I found eminent support for my conclusions in the following paragraph; it appears in the introduction to a translation of *The Aeneid* by a British poet, the late Cecil Day Lewis:

"A translation cannot be poetry in its own right unless it has been subdued to the imaginative process of its original; nor can it be a faithful translation unless it is in some sense an original poem. Only through such paradoxes can we see into the mystique of translating."

The Insoluble Problem

There come times in the life of a man when his egotism receives an unexpected jolt, which shakes him to question his assumption of omnipotence. These experiences are both painful and humbling, since they bring home sharply the realization that the will, after repeated failure, has reached its limits, and that to accomplish his intentions he must seek some untried means in order to escape from what had grown to be a consuming compulsion.

The mere recognition of his hopeless entrapment, as he meditates, induces the first step in a process of liberation which will lead perhaps unwittingly to his eventual escape. The imprisoning tensions will gradually lose their potency, and as body and brain recover their natural rhythms other considerations will intervene, little by little, to engage the attention. Once more will the mind take in the affairs of the everyday world, and although the problem will still remain unsolved, it will no longer overwhelm its victim.

In brief, what has been here described is a psychological transformation, from an involuntary subjective condition to one that is objective, and therefore controlled, detached, and seen in its true perspective. The change represents the conquest of the neurosis, the recovery of sanity, a restoration of the will and a revival of hope.

In support of this interpretation one may invoke the authority of eminence with two brief excerpts:

We believe that according to our desire we are able to change the things round about us; we believe this because otherwise we can see no favorable solution. . . . We do not succeed in changing things according to our desire, but gradually our desire changes. The situation that we hoped to change because it was intolerable becomes unimportant.

—Proust, *Remembrance of Things Past*

Some higher or wider interest arose on the person's horizon, and through this widening of his view the unsoluble problem lost its urgency. It was not solved logically on its own terms, but faded out in contrast to a new and stronger life-tendency. It was not repressed and made unconscious, but merely appeared in a different light, and so became different itself.

—Jung, *The Secret of the Golden Flower*

My Athletic Period

I don't know whatever impelled me—as I look back, it doesn't make sense—but there was a time in my teens when I harbored the ambition to shine as a track athlete, notably as a runner.

The reason I say it doesn't make sense is that both physically and temperamentally I lacked what it takes; I hadn't the makings.

The other evening, rummaging through a drawerful of adolescent memorabilia, I unearthed a photo of myself, dressed for competitive sport. On its back was the faded notation: "C.G.S. 1895." C.G.S. was short for Columbia Grammar School, where I prepared for college. In 1895 I was sixteen years old.

The picture squares with my memory: a run-of-the-mill teen-ager; height, five two, at most; weight, at a guess, under one hundred and twenty pounds.

But what also emerges from the dim print is a disqualifying disability impossible to correct—a pair of legs too short to co-ordinate with an expanding torso. I was consequently foredoomed to failure.

Why this discrepancy had escaped the notice of my gymnasium instructor I fail to understand. His name was Whewell; Mr. Whewell, an energetic Scotsman, had been in charge of my physique for nearly two years; for two hours each week he would conscientiously direct my exercises on chin-ups, the rings, the parallel bars, and all the other equipment of his workshop. He certainly kept me on my toes. I can still hear his barking voice urging me to "reep [for rip] into it," as I followed, at times falteringly, his strenuous commands.

And it was Mr. Whewell who practically insisted that I come out for the winter indoor interscholastics as a member of the school squad, to compete in the dashes.

The participants in the interscholastics were drawn chiefly from a group of private, proprietary schools in the neighborhood of C.G.S. and located in an oblong running from Forty-second to Fifty-ninth streets, bounded by Park and Sixth avenues. I still remember a few of their names—Drisler, Cutler, Berkeley, Barnard, Yale, Wilson and Kellogg. They flourished most prosperously during the eighteen-nineties, when the district was still solidly residential, but they succumbed one by one as business moved in and took over, and the old brownstone families moved out.

The interscholastic games were held on Saturday afternoons through the winter months in the various regimental armories of Manhattan and Brooklyn. Necessarily omitted from competition were the distance runs, from the mile to the hundred-yarder. Floor space barely permitted the fifty-yard straightaway, my "specialty," but once, in a Brooklyn armory, they actually were able to include a *sixty*-yard event, the final distance achieved out of the main area through an alcove into an anteroom.

In all of these meets I was a faithful but hapless contestant, my sole triumph a victory in a preliminary heat quickly erased the next time around.

My experience as a sprinter lasted long enough to destroy any illusion that I could make good in that role, and so, wiser but not wholly disheartened, I withdrew as a public performer for more sedentary tasks such as turning out jingles for the school paper.

Nevertheless I continued my hours—they were compulsory—at the gym under the eye of my undaunted instructor. To my surprise Mr. Whewell still professed his faith in my athletic future.

"Your legs weren't built for speed," he admitted in his plaid dialect, "but there's good material here to work with," poking me in the diaphragm. "Your lungs are strong, chest development better than average, and your respiration, if you keep to a steady clip, will give you the staying power for the long run. It's the staying power that's important. No," he went on, "it's not been a waste of time. You're past stage-fright and you've learned to compete."

I could see what this flattering testimonial was leading up to: to induce me to return to the arena in some other capacity, this time as a candidate for the mile. He was, in his crafty way, turning my mind to the Annual Field Day games to be held in early May at Columbia Oval, to the north of the city, at Williamsbridge.

I confess, with embarrassment, that the lure which had drawn me to the armories still held me captive, defying all logic, for one more try, this time out-of-doors.

And so, the next time I went to the gym, I told Mr. Whewell I was thinking of the mile event. "Fine," he said, definitely pleased. "You'll have about three weeks to train for it; you'll need all of that to work up your wind."

I agreed, and he took down my name as an entry in the mile.

In the year 1895 I lived with my parents and two younger

brothers on Seventieth Street, just off Lexington Avenue. C.G.S. was then located on Fifty-first Street, between Park and Madison avenues, a healthy mile between. In good weather I walked both ways, thereby saving two carfares, a nickel each. And now, with the stimulus of my new commitment, these daily walks turned into sturdy jogs. On the weekends I left the streets for more extended and unobstructed stretches over in Central Park.

By the end of the training period I felt a definite gain in both endurance and performance, particularly after surviving a preliminary test at the quarter-mile oval on the eve of the meet. I knew, however, it would take every ounce of stamina to sustain me in the excitement of a competition which I was to experience for the first time, and with unknown contenders.

On page 12 of the program of events, which I still cherish, I read: "One Mile Run (handicap)," and find six names, including my own. G. E. Kittle was the only one listed for scratch. He was in the form above me and had been a winner the year before. The handicaps ranged from thirty to sixty yards. My own discount of fifty yards indicated that those in charge of the gradings felt more charitable to at least one other contestant. On what had they based their estimates? Surely not on my painful showing in the armory games. But might they not have considered with some degree of favor my management of the distance in my practice lope around the oval? In any case a fifty-yards allowance might turn out to be useful toward being placed at the finish.

All I now remember of the natural scene is the state of the weather. This May day was one of James Russell

Lowell's days in June, gentle, sunny, a clear invitation to be out in the open.

Our event was slated for the late afternoon. Meanwhile the other contests were moving along according to schedule, many of them no longer to be found in today's competitions. In the one-mile bicycle race, to illustrate, the two wheels of the vehicle, antedating today's safety model, consisted of a high wheel with a step to reach the seat and a very small one to balance, at the rear. Then there was the mile walk, not the natural pedestrian gait but an artificial heel-and-toe operation, to be pursued without change or relaxation of pace to the finish. This has been revived in a modified form.

Quite understandable was the proviso, since only the first three counted for medals, that no event would be started without at least four participants. When our turn came around, the original entries had been reduced from six to five; one boy failed to show up. Anyway, the proviso didn't concern us.

At last we lined up. I found my place in the middle lane, overshadowed between two giants whose extra inches emphasized the height I lacked and needed. Then, at pistol-crack we were off, only to be called back because one fellow had jumped the gun. (His infraction, unlike a similar break-through in the line of a modern football game, carried no penalty.)

For the better part of the first lap we remained closely bunched, Kittle setting what amounted to a companionable pace. Soon, however, he made it a more serious affair, gradually stepping up the tempo. By the time we all had circled the track the second time, Kittle had steadily widened the yardage between himself and the next man. At the end of the third round he had eaten up our handicaps. It was all too plain that no one would be able to overtake him.

For at least three of us the possibility of winning the race had long since evaporated. Survival now became a simple matter of staying power, and that meant to keep one's head and not be panicked, to plod on however slowly, and to continue to hold the rhythm of a steady clip with regular breathing. In short, to make the most of "Professor" Whewell's admonitions.

So far I had been performing respectably and had even managed to move up to—and hold on to—fourth place, with boy number five no longer a threat. But now, with less than half a lap still to go, I suddenly weakened, stumbled over my own feet, and narrowly escaped a fall. The shock, by an odd bit of luck, helped me to gain my second wind and keep in the running.

And then—was it a miracle or serendipity—the boy ahead of me suddenly staggered dizzily and rolled off onto the grass.

Seconds later, I crossed the finish line.

Now, some seventy-eight years from that famous day, I hold in my hand a bronze medal—a classical goddess, suitably garbed for the occasion, bestows a wreath of bay or laurel upon an unseen hero for whom no room is left on the disc. Time has treated it kindly; it has lost none of its original freshness or luster, as it dangles from a light blue-and-white silk badge.

It is this emblem which marks the end of my eventful athletic period.

The Houdini I Knew

In the first quarter of this century two names, one of a character in a novel, the other of a performing artist, became, because of their symbolic characteristics, incorporated in our common speech and acceptable by dictionaries as permanent additions to the English language.

The first was Babbitt, the bromidic, heart-land hero of the Sinclair Lewis novel of that name; the second was Houdini, master-magician, conjuror, pre-eminent as an escapist in extricating himself from seemingly foolproof devices of restraint and confinement.

The phrase "to do a Houdini" was quickly adopted to signify a person's cunning in succeeding in a situation against apparently hopeless odds.

These two names come to mind together since both Sinclair Lewis and Harry Houdini were clients of our law firm. The present essay, however, will be confined to my recollections of Houdini.

It must have been around the years 1910 or 1911 that we met for the first time. He had come to the office late in the afternoon to consult my partner, Bernard Ernst, on some legal matter. Their session lasted well beyond regular office hours, for when it was over and Ernst introduced us, I was the only one still around.

In those early days of our partnership we were modestly installed in a building, long since demolished, on Liberty Street between Nassau and William. It ran through to

Maiden Lane but its main entrance was on the Liberty Street side; to leave by way of Maiden Lane one had to descend a flight of three or four steps, since that exit was at a lower level because of a slope in the terrain.

We stepped off the elevator at the Liberty Street floor onto a deserted corridor, its main electric lighting already turned off. Ernst ran ahead, while we lingered in the semidarkness, only to report that we were locked in. As I started toward the other way out, Houdini called: "Hold it! First let me check."

In less than a minute of fiddling with a gimmick he had with him, he managed to hit on the Open Sesame, led us into the street, and then, proudly and conscientiously, made fast the doors as he had found them.

We parted at the next corner to go our separate ways. Although few words had passed between Houdini and myself during this first brief encounter, they proved sufficient to lead to a solid unbroken friendship.

A visit of Houdini to our office meant general suspension of work until he left, since he needed little coaxing to put on an act with whatever material might lie around to attract his interest and enlist his skills. I recall the day when a stenographer challenged him to open the office safe. He walked over to it, inspected it gravely, and then, with pretended caution, said: "I've worked on many safes, but I've never seen one like this; it looks like an antique: it's a monument."

It was indeed both an antique and a monument, a product of a cruder era, which we had bought second-hand when we started out. I think it was a Mosler. It possessed aesthetic as well as utilitarian values. Its heavy iron doors were dec-

orated with an oil painting of some Currier and Ives scene—
it may have been a Mississippi river-boat—a specimen of
early-nineteenth-century Americana which should ultimately have found a home in a museum or the Smithsonian
Institution as an example of a prevailing type of commercial
art.

I never could remember the combination on the disc
between its handles and needed a note to refer to before I
could venture to deal with it. It had a clock-face dial, to be
twirled four times, right and left, to the necessary numerals
before the final click. We gathered closely around Houdini
as he set to work. If he used any tool beyond his dexterous
fingers, I failed to detect it. Previous experience must have
prepared him for this four-way maneuver. He twiddled
around for some time, whether it was really necessary or
merely to impress us with his seeming difficulties, and then
he pulled the doors apart.

I should perhaps explain my general attitude toward the
art of prestidigitation in contrast to that of my partner,
Ernst. To me the simplest trick was as incomprehensible as
those more difficult and dangerous; the release of a live
rabbit or dove from a conjuror's empty hands, or the underwater escape to dry land from a nailed and trussed packing-
case I found equally baffling. The satisfactions these won-
ders evoked lay purely in their entertainment values, which
proved highly fascinating and enjoyable. But there the
matter rested. My curiosity was never sufficiently stirred or
involved to attempt solutions.

Ernst, on the other hand, must have been born with the
love of magic in his blood. As a boy he had made it a
favorite hobby. Soon he became an amateur of parts, enter-

taining his friends with his parlor tricks. In time he qualified as a member of the Society of American Magicians and finally succeeded to the presidency. It was as fellow-workers in the Society that he and Houdini first met, took to each other, and formed what turned out to be a life-long friendship. And so, what began as a boy's pastime ultimately grew to an absorbing, satisfying avocation.

Ernst's promotion to an unsalaried presidency carried with it time-consuming responsibilities which he freely discharged at our office. Occasionally, however, he might also be consulted professionally.

I hold before me a photograph of Houdini standing next to his friend Sir Arthur Conan Doyle. The latter, a six-footer-and-over, emphasizes by contrast a difference of at least five inches in their height. Houdini stands no taller than five eight, the average male stature at the beginning of the century. It is summer. Doyle is topped with a flat straw boater; Houdini is wearing a light "ice-cream" suit, predecessor of our present seersucker. His hair is parted down the middle, the style of the period. Beyond a pair of piercing eyes, nothing in the picture hints at the personality of the individual behind them.

It was indeed a complex personality. Uppermost to the public view was the consummate showman, who had won supremacy in his profession and captured his world-wide audiences only after years of self-discipline, self-denial, and study. The ability to arrive at this eminence and sustain it down to his untimely death must have sprung from the legitimate egotism and tenacity of the dedicated artist, an egotism which so often undermines acceptance and popularity.

But Houdini's egotism was interwoven and spiced with a winning charm and a liberal supply of humor. To those who knew him off the stage and out of the limelight he was a genial, warm-hearted companion, essentially a serious person. His early marriage to Beatrice Rahner prospered happily and devotedly for the rest of his fifty-two years. Bess served him as the helpful assistant, supplying the accessories for his performances and working at times as a confederate in his mystifications. There were no children. Knowing his affectionate nature, I wondered how seriously the lack may have influenced his life.

An odd, amusing quirk, which brought us closer together, was his fascination with twins, whose birth he apparently regarded as one of nature's special miracles. This came home to me one day in the autumn of 1910 when I announced to him I had just become the father of identical twin daughters. He responded excitedly to the news and from that day on, when writing on tour, would send his love to "the famous Connecticut twins." He would also from time to time mail me clippings from local newspapers which had something fresh to print on the subject.

My daughters were in their third year when Houdini saw them for the first time. It was the period when my wife, taking them out for a walk, would be stopped by strangers who would ask: "How can you tell them apart?"

But Houdini's scrutiny, more mischievously directed, was rewarded by the very fact of their likeness to each other. Something evidently was working, unspoken, behind a mysterious smile. Noticing a trace of embarrassment, I broke the silence with "Tell us what's on your mind."

"A wicked thought," he answered. "You know my trick of sawing a woman in half? Well, I've never tried it with identical twins."

Our failure to respond was not encouraging; even had it been, he would never have pursued the idea, for when he next saw them, a year later, they had already developed physical differences sufficient to disqualify them.

This memoir aims to serve as a fair record of a personal relationship which covers over fifteen years. It also makes note of certain reactions and impressions arising not only out of that relationship but also from a larger consideration of the development of a singular individual. The over-all Houdini story one finds most completely and authoritatively presented in the biography by Harold Kellock, published originally in 1930; it is supported by material supplied by Mrs. Houdini, her accumulated note-takings and diaries of their life together.

As I reflect on Houdini's career, from its unpromising start to its ripe fulfillment, I find that he truly deserves the term—so often used without warrant—the self-made man.

Born Ehrich Weiss, son of an orthodox rabbi, he ran away from his Wisconsin home at the age of twelve years, whether out of momentary pique or from a youngster's yearning for adventure. The latter conjecture seems the more likely.

It was the lure of a tenth-rate circus passing through the town that sent him on his way. He entered the magical world of entertainment as a water-boy for the animals.

I characterize Houdini as the authentic self-made man, since it was the discovery of his inner resources and his steadfast determination to make the most of them that accounts for his high stature, both technically, as an artist, and spiritually, as a compassionate human being.

His ambition drove him beyond the satisfactions of popular acclaim; it ran deeper, as a moral compulsion to utilize his average male body to the limit of its capacity—a challenge calling for unremitting disciplines and sacrifice. He would undergo the most taxing tests, such as running ever increasing distances or swimming for long periods in icy rushing streams, in order to gain that muscular flexibility, respiratory power, and all-round dexterity and control without which the performance of his seemingly superhuman feats, such as his underwater escape from a packing-box, would have been impossible.

Houdini always kept in training, his restless energies ever active with fresh experiments and new exercises. I am reminded of an evening at his home on West 113th Street, near Columbia University. After dinner we moved to the living room and had hardly settled down when Houdini quietly removed his shoes and socks and produced a stout cord which he threw carelessly on the floor in front of him. Then he put the big toe of his right foot to work on the cord. He wriggled it as deftly as if he were using his fingers, drawing together the two ends, twisting them into a loop and finally twining them into a firm knot.

But soon the evening took on a more serious and unexpected turn. As I yielded to the atmosphere of the room lined with its book-filled shelves I realized I was in the presence of an individual far more complex and purposeful than the spectacular headliner at the Palace, the Hippodrome, and Hammerstein's Victoria Roof—the show-off whose photograph headed his stationery, and who signed himself imperially, like Napoleon, with a single name.

These volumes represented the solid research of years into the history of legerdemain as practiced by his predecessors in the United States and other countries; a study which Houdini held indispensable for his own education.

He was an insatiable collector of letters and diaries of famous magicians and mediums, and his investigations led him into the world of psychic phenomena and culminated in the creation of great libraries in both fields.

As the evening flew on and Houdini revealed his inner self ever more freely to his absorbed listener, the significance of his achievement grew the more amazing. What was being disclosed in the quiet room was a feat surpassing the most daring and incredible of his vaudeville exploits; it was the transformation of an uneducated runaway lad into a dedicated scholar.

It was after midnight when my visit came to an end. The unrestrained, intimate disclosures of my host revealed a depth of character and range of interest unsuspected in our casual meetings.

Moving into middle age, along with his role as a performing artist Houdini took upon himself a second, weightier career, an investigation into the domain of the spirit, speculating on the existence of an afterlife and of communication from and with the dead. It may well be conjectured that a contributing influence for his choice of subject was an overpowering attachment to his dead mother, in life his dearest confidante, to whose loss he was never to become reconciled. (His first impulse on returning from a tour was to visit her grave in filial devotion.)

His natural inclination, accordingly, would be to hope for the survival of the spirit.

To equip himself for the project he began by reading widely and deeply in the literature of psychic phenomena, but he discovered before long that the recording of past events merely served as background for his task and had no probative value. He must rely on his own first-hand observations, which would require attendance at the séances of trance mediums whenever an opportunity might offer. This set him on a time-consuming pursuit which was to become a major involvement and from which he accumulated the material to be studied. At many of the sessions he recognized the "medium" as a former magician whose "effects" emanated from a source somewhat below the supernatural.

In such cases he would rise from his chair, confront the impostor, and proceed to demolish him—or her, it was often a woman—by revealing to the audience the techniques of the deception. The traffic in fake communication with the dead rose with America's entry into World War I in 1917, as the lists of those struck down in battle lengthened.

Nevertheless there were other occasions on which the character of the revelations lay beyond his endeavor to account for them. Neither, in all fairness, could he reject them, or bar out their conceivability as authentic manifestations. A further body of material for his study grew out of conversations and discussions with individuals claiming to have experienced personal proof of existence beyond the material world. A firm adherent to this belief was his friend Sir Arthur Conan Doyle. A lively presentation of their opposing views resulted in a lengthy exchange of letters, later edited by Bernard Ernst and Hereward Carrington, and published in 1932 under the title *Houdini and Conan Doyle*. It was Doyle's belief that Houdini possessed psychic force and that he wanted to believe in the afterlife; Doyle, on the other hand, firmly asserted: "I *know* that spirit return is a fact." To the end of his days Houdini entertained the wish if not the hope. He had made a promise to Bessie, in all sincerity, to speak to her from beyond the grave, and year after year his widow, Bessie, would wait in vain for the promise to be kept.

In a volume entitled *A Magician Among the Spirits* Houdini published his adventures with mediums. The work, not unexpectedly, drew sharply diametric reactions from believers and skeptics.

On one point, however, there could be no disagreement, but only praise and admiration: Houdini's unselfish service in exposing fraudulent séances and bringing to book the creatures who preyed and profited on the susceptibilities of the bereaved.

This accomplishment, while especially noteworthy, was not unique, but true to character; it merely emphasized Houdini's innate concern for the unfortunate and the hopeless. Houdini was always the public-spirited citizen, generous with time and money, responsive to every call.

On the national level he toured across the country on a Liberty-bond-selling drive when the United States was drawn into World War I. It was on this drive that I had the good luck to see him do his mystifying underwater box-trick, the most hazardous of his ventures in freeing himself. It took place off-shore in Long Island Sound at Saugatuck, Connecticut, and will be referred to again later.

The intoxication of fame and fortune, so potent and corrupting to many whose ambition had propelled them to heights of power, never lessened Houdini's sympathies and helpfulness to friends of earlier days, especially fellow-magicians once in popular favor but now jobless and down on their luck.

As I think of Houdini, the magician, I recall above his other skills in deception his special proclivity to ways of escape, a perhaps unconscious hunger for freedom, not only of the flesh but conceivably of the spirit as well. And I am encouraged in this preference by the verdict of the general public, who are inclined to refer to him less as the conjuror of the Indian needle trick and the slicer of a live human body than, in capital letters, as "THE GREAT ESCAPE ARTIST" or "THE HANDCUFF KING."

His first escape, by no means magical, was no less cunningly planned and effectively executed. It was prompted not by a sense of imminent danger but, refreshingly, by a small boy's wanderlust for wider horizons. It had to be done swiftly and by stealth; disclosure to his parents would have been fatal, for he was not in revolt against them, but a loving and dutiful son. His getaway created no break in their relations and, once a safe distance from pursuit, he wrote home reassuringly of his whereabouts and, by doing so, started a correspondence destined to continue unbroken for the rest of his life.

His concern for their needs and comforts became a foremost responsibility from the time of his earliest scanty pay checks, which he shared with them.

Meanwhile, the life at Appleton, Wisconsin, held no promise of easier, more rewarding days. The congregation of Rabbi Weiss, small, diminishing, and close to poverty, could offer him little more than an honorarium in return for his devotion and self-sacrifice.

Finally, driven to desperation, he confided in his young son Ehrich, still in his teens, who had drifted to New York to take a boring job as a tie-cutter, while spending his free hours more fruitfully in preparing for his future career.

Ehrich's response was unhesitant, not merely with sympathy but with immediate action. He quickly arranged to have his father join him in New York and leave the rabbinate and Appleton for good. The old man, well into his sixties, soon shared a bench with his son and added his frugal earnings to their joint economy during his few surviving years. It was only after Ehrich the tie-cutter had become transformed into Houdini the rising magician that his income proved sufficient to support and complete his youthful dream of uniting the family under one roof and in a more promising environment. At first he could do no more than move them out of their village home into a cramped walk-up flat in a city slum neighborhood. But with his increasing popularity and affluence as a world-wide artist, their living conditions steadily improved. And when Harry and Bess decided in their middle years to buy the house on 113th Street, a main consideration was to provide a permanent residence for his aging mother and her other children.

Despite the long years of travel on extended professional tours over three continents, Houdini lives in one's mind as a home-maker and family man.

Houdini's final tour was cut short by a shocking accident, incurred not as a performer failing in a stage act—his record was clear—but from a totally unforeseeable source. It was due to his propensity for issuing challenges, whether to other conjurors to duplicate his tricks, or to unmask an impostor by proving that a claimed communication with another world was merely the product of his more earthly invention as an illusionist.

But the challenge on that late day in October fell into neither of these categories and was not even remotely concerned with magic or sorcery. On that day Houdini was playing a combination magic-and-lecture date in Montreal, Canada. During the intermission he was resting in his dressing room, relaxed and naked on a cot, when two students from the audience, eager fans from McGill University, entered unannounced for an interview. Without warning, one of the young men landed a series of stout blows on his abdomen. Houdini collapsed, overcome by the fierce pain, but, after a brief delay, insisted on completing his engagement. (The show must go on!)

The heartbroken young man had ignored the conditions of the challenge, which was that Houdini prepare himself in advance for any attack. This challenge he could make with the assurance that he had developed his stomach muscles to such a degree of tension and rigidity as to be immune to the most terrific punch. It was a challenge never successfully invoked.

The account of Houdini's last days need but brief recording, since it was so fully reported at the time. His condition grew worse the next day. He completed his performance with great difficulty. It was only during the following week, after stubbornly continuing his tour to Detroit, that he collapsed and consented to surgery. The operation disclosed a ruptured appendix, impaired beyond recovery.

The date was October 31, 1926.

It was hard to become reconciled to the reality that Houdini would never visit our office again. As the days passed the memory of his presence lingered on, somewhat disturbingly in my own case. An unconscious impulse to speak with him might strike me without warning and leave me baffled. Months went by without any adjustment to his loss. My troubled state at length began to define itself when it dawned on me that unfinished business remained to be transacted, that I should be doing something about it in some way and that I had a debt to discharge before I could hope to regain peace of mind.

I began to ask myself questions to determine how best to proceed. If I was destined by fate no longer to speak with Houdini, nothing prevented me from speaking eagerly and warmly about him. It should take some form of a written remembrance.

This decided, I set to work and before long found myself deeply engaged. It was to be a portrait sketch, a poem rather than a prose piece, as such lines as the following came to me out of the blue:

"To slip the strait-jacket of the flesh," and
　　"To do the box-trick in water,
　　when the July sun is shining,
　　is hard,
　　but harder still,
　　on a cold November day
　　to swim through clay."

After almost an entire year of experiment, false starts, frustrations, and eliminations, I preserved some ninety-three lines and assembled them into the following arrangement:

Houdini

The papers said:
"Houdini Dead!"
Racing newsboys yelled:
"Houdini dead! Houdini dead!"
People read, smiled:
"Just another front
Page publicity stunt."
But Houdini *was* dead.

How can one get away with it,—
The box-trick,—
How can one fool Death?

No one could fix the committee,
An undertaker, chairman.
Dead men play no tricks,
But was he "playing dead"?
How could a dead magician
Put it over a live mortician?

They clamped him with manacles,
Shackled his ankles,
Clapped him in a case,
Strapped him to his place,
Locked the lid.

He did what he was bid.
They kept the watch by day,
They vigiled him by night
In the sputtering candle-light.
He never left their sight.

They bore him from the house,
They caged him in a hearse
(The hearse was framed in glass,
Was screwed with screws of brass,
And only light could pass).

They took him for a ride,
Captive, chained and tied;
They set him on the ground,
Coffined, fettered, bound,—
The damp November ground.
He made no sound.

The grave was dark and deep,
The walls were high and steep;
They lifted him and lowered him,
They shoveled earth, a heavy heap—
A rising heap, a dwindling hole.
A rabbi made a prayer for his soul.

II

Years ago, a mid-summer day,
Saugatuck, Long Island Sound.
Suddenly he stepped out on the shore,
Dropped his robe,

A bather,
Smiling, bowing, in the sun.
Incredulous ones
Peered within a packing case,
Felt for secret panels,
Tapped each side.
Strangers tied him, hand and foot and torse,
Hammered fast the top with nails of steel,
Roped and double-roped and tugged the knots.
A high derrick dipped,
An iron hook slipped,
Clinched the rope,
Pulled its dangling burden clear of land,
Plunged it in the waves.
Then, as it rose again, a swinging minute,
A swimmer stroked his triumph toward the bank.

To do the box-trick in water,
When the July sun is shining,
Is hard;
But, harder still,
On a cold November day
To swim through clay.

III

This was no mountebank,
No spangled juggler
Of rubber-balls and billiard cues and lamps—
This was and is and ever will be spirit.
There is a legerdemain
Unsensed by mortal fingers,

A clairvoyance
The perishable brain
Is hopeless to attain.
There is a heart-beat of the spirit;
No one can time it.
There is a blood, a muscle, of the soul.
Lithe is the spirit and nimble
To loose the cords of the body;
Wiry and supple the soul
To slip the strait-jacket of the flesh.

IV

Out of an unbroken grave,
Above unheeding mourners,
Before the sightless eyes of conjurors,
Houdini rose
And lightly sprinted down an aisle of air
Amid the relieved and welcoming applause
Of those already there.

First published in *Harper's Magazine*, July, 1928.

Index of Titles